SLOTHS

James Maclaine

Illustrated by Maribel Lechuga
Additional illustrations by Bonnie Pang
Designed by Claire Morgan and Sam Whibley

Sloth consultant: Professor David Macdonald CBE,
Wildlife Conservation Research Unit, Zoology Department, University of Oxford
Reading consultant: Alison Kelly

Contents

All sloths have three toes on their legs. Their arms have either two or three toes.

Upside down

Sloths live in warm, wet forests in Central and South America.

They hang upside down in trees.

So slow

When sloths move, they're very, very slow.

A sloth lifts just one of its arms when it starts to move.

It grabs a branch before moving its legs across too.

Then the sloth moves its other arm and climbs up slowly.

This sloth is resting on top of a branch.

Sloths sometimes sit in trees instead of hanging.

Even sloths' eyelids move slowly when they blink.

Sloth fur

Sloths have a thick layer of fur under lots of long, shaggy hairs.

This sloth is brushing its fur with its claws.

When sloths hang,
their hairs point down.
This helps rainwater
to drip off.

If you looked closely
at a sloth, you'd spot
lots of moths living
in its fur.

Over 100 moths can be found
on a single sloth.

Turning green

Tiny plants called algae grow in sloths' fur. Algae grows better when it's wet.

In dry weather, the algae in a sloth's fur looks brown.

The algae starts to turn green at rainy times each year.

As more algae grows, the sloth gets greener. This helps it to hide from dangerous eagles.

There is lots of algae on this brown-throated sloth.

When it's dry again, the algae will fade.

Finding their way

Sloths can't see very well. They use smell and touch so they know where to climb.

A sloth finds its way to the top of a tree to lie in sunlight.

If it gets too hot, the sloth moves in search of shade.

Sometimes a sloth feels its way along a vine between two trees. Sloths can't jump.

This sloth is
bending its neck to
sniff in a different direction.

Three-toed sloths twist their
necks much further than you can.

Going down

Sloths spend very little time
on or near the ground.

If a sloth lives by
a river, it goes
down to drink.

It dangles from roots
above the water.

Sloths sometimes move across the forest floor to get to a different tree.

A sloth climbs down a tree trunk bottom first.

When it reaches the ground, it starts to crawl.

It takes the sloth a long time to reach the next tree.

Leaf eaters

Sloths mostly eat leaves, stems and fruit that grow on different trees.

A maned sloth grabs a leafy branch and pulls it to its mouth to eat.

The sloth bites a leaf with its hard lips. Then it uses its teeth to chew and chew.

Two-toed sloths sometimes eat insects and little lizards too.

This brown-throated sloth has found
a tasty, red bud to eat.

Sloth poop

Sloths poop once a week.

This sloth is pooping
next to a tree.

Sloths only
poop on
the ground.

The poop is important for the moths that live on sloths.

Female moths leave the sloth to lay their eggs inside its poop.

When the eggs hatch, the baby moths eat the poop.

After growing wings, the young moths fly up to find the sloth.

Sloth fight

Adult sloths live on their own. They try to keep away from other sloths.

An adult male sloth chases any other males that he meets.

As the sloth gets closer, he starts to swipe with his claws.

If the sloths fight, they bite and scratch one another.

These two sloths are wrestling on a branch.

They'll keep fighting until one of them falls to the ground.

Sloths can drop from high up without getting hurt.

Baby sloths

Mother sloths have their babies while hanging from trees. Each mother has only one baby at a time.

When a baby sloth is born, the mother licks it clean.

The baby already has fur and claws. It can open its eyes too.

The baby clings to its mother's tummy and drinks her milk.

This mother sloth's baby is now
two months old.

Growing up

Young sloths stay close to their mothers as they grow up.

This mother sloth is teaching her baby which types of leaves it can eat.

Every young sloth
keeps holding onto
its mother until it
learns how to climb.

At first, it tries to
hang by its arms
while sitting
on its mother.

Then it starts to
climb on its own.
It will leave its
mother after a year.

Strong swimmers

Sloths are surprisingly good at swimming.

Sometimes floods happen where sloths live. Rivers overflow and cover the ground.

To move between trees, a sloth has to swim. First, it climbs into the water.

Then the sloth floats on its tummy. It uses its arms to paddle quickly.

This is a pygmy three-toed sloth.

It's swimming in the sea near a forest.

Baby sloths ride on their mothers' backs in water.

Sloth sounds

Sloths mostly keep quiet, but they can make noises for different reasons.

A sloth hisses at another sloth to tell it to keep away.

If an eagle attacks, a sloth tries to scare it off by growling.

When a female sloth wants to attract male sloths, she makes loud noises.

If a baby sloth falls
out of a tree, it calls
for its mother.

Meeeeep

Meeeeep

The baby keeps bleating so the
mother knows where to find it.

Fast asleep

Sloths sleep for about ten hours every day.

This sloth is leaning back to snooze.

Sloths can hang by their arms and legs even as they sleep.

Sometimes a sleepy sloth curls up into a ball. It rests its head on its chest.

Two-toed sloths climb in between tangles of vines and then fall asleep.

Both three-toed sloths and two-toed sloths are often awake at night.

Glossary

Here are some of the words in this book you might not know. This page tells you what they mean.

 eyelid - a thin fold of skin. Eyelids cover eyes when they're closed.

 claw - a long, sharp nail. Sloths use their claws to hang, climb and fight.

 moth - a type of insect. Some moths live on sloths.

 algae - tiny types of plants. Green algae grows in sloths' fur.

 eagle - a large bird. Some eagles try to catch sloths to eat.

 vine - a type of plant. Vines are long and thin. They grow around trees.

 flood - a very large amount of water. Floods cover dry land.

Usborne Quicklinks

Would you like to find out more about sloths, and watch them climb through the treetops? Visit Usborne Quicklinks for links to websites with videos, facts and activities.

Go to **usborne.com/Quicklinks** and type in the keywords "**beginners sloths**." Make sure you ask a grown-up before going online.

Notes for grown-ups

Please read the internet safety guidelines at Usborne Quicklinks with your child. Children should be supervised online. The websites are regularly reviewed and the links at Usborne Quicklinks are updated. However, Usborne Publishing is not responsible and does not accept liability for the content or availability of any website other than its own.

This pygmy three-toed sloth lives on an island in the Caribbean Sea. Pygmy three-toed sloths can be found nowhere else in the world.